·OYÈRE

AVIATION ARCHAEOLOGY
IN BRITAIN

SHIRE ARCHAEOLOGY

2

British Library Cataloguing in Publication Data: De la Bédoyère, Guy
Aviation archaeology in Britain. – (Shire archaeology; 80)
1. Aircraft accidents – Great Britain
2. World War, 1939-1945 – Aerial operations
3. Excavations (Archaeology)
I. Title 941'.084
ISBN 0 7478 0490 7

Published in 2001 by
SHIRE PUBLICATIONS LTD
Cromwell House, Church Street, Princes Risborough,
Buckinghamshire HP27 9AA, UK.
(Website: www.shirebooks.co.uk)

Series Editor: James Dyer.

Number 80 in the Shire Archaeology series.

ISBN 0 7478 0490 7.

First published 2001.

Printed in Great Britain by
CIT Printing Services Ltd, Press Buildings,
Merlins Bridge, Haverfordwest, Pembrokeshire SA61 1XF.

Contents

List of illustrations

Foreword and acknowledgements

Britain has one of the richest archaeological and historical heritages in the world, ranging from the mists of remote prehistory in the form of monuments like Stonehenge to the great medieval buildings like Canterbury Cathedral and Edinburgh Castle. The path through history includes Roman monuments such as Hadrian's Wall and a host of other remarkable places testifying to man's exploitation of a fertile and strategically located island. Ever since the days of the late eighteenth century, Britain's past has been explored by archaeologists who have developed all sorts of ways of understanding it.

Heritage took a new turn in south-east England when the area became the front line in the air war of 1939–45. The consequences of that war produced a new stratum of archaeology, spreading right across the whole of Britain. Scattered everywhere are the crash sites of fighters and bombers, along with the derelict remains of airfields.

In the twenty-first century much of what is left in the ground is steadily decaying, though a small army of aviation enthusiasts have established a series of museums. At once evocative and provocative, aviation archaeology has become a dynamic movement in the preservation of Britain's heritage. It has proved controversial but without it we would now have little physical record of this most vital period in Britain's history. The RAF Memorial Museum at Manston, Kent, is now one of the most popular museums in the region, testifying to the great interest in this period at a time when living memory is starting to fade.

This book is an attempt to introduce a wider readership to aviation archaeology and some of the issues surrounding it. What is particularly interesting is, firstly, how the combination of archaeological techniques and deposits can be linked with the documentary record of the period. This provides an opportunity to test theories, as well as to reconstruct the unique events making up each incident. Such things are rarely available to the archaeologist, who is normally obliged to fall back on generalities to explain features. Secondly, aviation archaeology at the present time resembles much of the antiquarian archaeology of the eighteenth and nineteenth centuries. The enthusiasm, interest and private resources have been vital to the preservation of this period while at the same time there has had to be a rapid learning curve to develop techniques.

I should like to thank Peter Kirk of the Rolls-Royce Heritage Trust for his help and advice concerning the Rolls-Royce engines of the era, and also, for answering a variety of queries: Colin Lee, Ian MacLachlan,

Simon Parry, Andy Saunders, Steve Vizard, John Manning, and the curatorial staff at Lashenden Air Warfare Museum, all of whom have been involved in different aspects of aviation archaeology for many years, as well as Simon Raikes and Jeremy Cross for inviting me to participate in two aviation excavations filmed for television. I should also like to thank Rodger Connell for drawing my attention to a recent publication of records of No. 92 (East India) Squadron Spitfires at Croydon on 30th March 1940.

Guy de la Bédoyère, Welby, 2001

Glossary

B-17F / B-17G Flying Fortress: American four-engine high-altitude daylight heavy bomber (figures 12, 31, 34, 38, 44).

B-24 Liberator: American four-engine long-range daylight heavy bomber.

Beaufighter: twin-engine British fighter-bomber.

Defiant: British twin-seat single-engine fighter with rear-facing turret.

Dornier Do17: German twin-engine short-range bomber (figure 11).

Eighth (8th) Air Force: arm of the United States Army Air Forces allocated to daylight heavy bombing duties based in England. Divided into the First and Third Bombardment Wings (*B-17F / B-17G*) and Second Bombardment Wing (*B-24*), each subdivided into Bombardment Groups, further subdivided into Bomb Squadrons. Some fighter units were also attached.

Flying Fortress: see *B-17F / B-17G*.

Focke-Wulf Fw 190: German single *radial-engine* high performance fighter.

Halifax: British four-engine heavy bomber (figures 20, 26).

Heinkel He 111: German twin-engine bomber (figure 14).

Hurricane: British single-engine fighter armed with machine guns, and later cannon (figures 2, 5, 22, 23, 24, 30).

JG: *Jagdgeschwader* – German for fighter squadron.

Jumo 211: Junkers inverted (upside-down) twelve-cylinder (two banks of six) engine fitted to various German aircraft, such as the *Junkers Ju 87*, and *Junkers Ju 88* (figure 35).

Junkers Ju 87 Stuka: German single-engine two-man dive bomber (figure 1).

Junkers Ju 88: German twin-engine fighter-bomber.

KG: *Kampfgeschwader* – German for bomber squadron (figure 11).

Lancaster: British four-engine long-range heavy bomber, used by the RAF for night bombing (figure 53).

Liberator: see *B-24 Liberator*.

Merlin: Rolls-Royce *V-12* engine fitted to British machines such as the *Hurricane, Lancaster* and *Spitfire* (figures 2, 20, 21, 22, 24, 25, 36, 48).

Messerschmitt Bf 109: German single-engine fighter armed with machine guns and cannon.

Messerschmitt Bf 110: German twin-engine long-range fighter armed with machine guns and cannon (figure 10).

Monocoque: airframe design in which shaped surface metal skinning, riveted to a metal frame, bears most of the force. Used in the *Spitfire*, for example (figure 33).

Mosquito: British twin-engine high-speed wooden fighter-bomber (figure 48).

Mustang: see *P-51 Mustang*.

P-47 Thunderbolt: American single *radial-engine* heavy fighter used to escort bombers (figures 4, 27, 29).

P-51 Mustang: American single-engine long-range fighter used to escort bombers.

Radial engine: engine with cylinders arranged like a star, usually in one bank of nine (single row, see cover), or two banks of nine (twin row, figures 19, 27).

Spitfire: British single-engine fighter in production throughout the Second World War in various guises, armed with machine guns and later with cannon as well (figures 3, 6, 7, 15, 16, 18, 28, 32, 33, 36, 37, 52).

Stirling: British four-engine heavy bomber from the early part of the war. Later used as a glider tug.

Stuka: see *Junkers Ju 87*.

Supercharger: sealed unit in which the fuel–air mixture is forced to pass through narrow chambers by high-speed rotors. This elevates the pressure, and compensates for thin air at high altitude (figures 20, 21).

Thunderbolt: see *P-47 Thunderbolt*.

V-12: twelve-cylinder engine arranged in two banks of six resembling a V in profile (figures 21, 22, 24).

Wasp: American *radial engine*, usually twin-row, fitted to the *B-24* and *P-47* (figures 19, 27).

Werk/Werke: German for 'works number'; precedes aircraft's serial number.

Wright Cyclone: American single-row *radial engine* fitted to the *B-17F / B-17G* (cover, figure 44).

1
Introduction

During the Second World War (1939–45) an average of five aircraft crashed every day somewhere in the British Isles (figure 1). Nowadays such events are, thankfully, rare enough to mean that when they do happen they make national news. But aircraft end their lives in only a few ways. They are scrapped, put into museums, or they crash. The reasons for crashes are many but during a war they become even more numerous. Today, aviation is more tightly regulated. Pilot training is intensive and protracted, and aircraft themselves are safer than they have ever been.

When a nation's survival is at stake different conditions apply. In the Second World War thousands of aircraft were in the air every day, flown by men and women of different backgrounds, age and experience. Many pilots in command of powerful and heavily armed aircraft were in their early twenties or even late teens, regardless of whether they came from Britain, the United States of America, Canada, Australia, New Zealand, South Africa, Germany or Italy.

1. A Junkers Ju 87 (Stuka) two-man dive bomber crashes out of control on 18th August 1940. It smashed into the ground at West Broyle, near Chichester, West Sussex. Both crew were killed.

2. Kept in reserve during the Battle of Britain, Canadian-built Hurricane I, Z7010, was on a delivery flight to RAF Hullavington in Wiltshire on 17th March 1941 when the pilot lost control in 'completely unsuitable weather' (crash report). Although the machine was destroyed, killing the pilot, in an accessible location near Princes Risborough, Buckinghamshire, the engine was left underground, from where it was recovered many years later.

Crews were asked to fly their machines vast distances, heavily laden, and sometimes under appalling conditions. Collisions were common and inevitable, especially when tight formations were being maintained in dense cloud. Even navigational training exercises could take aircraft and their crews into unspeakable weather across western Britain, while a flight planned to do no more than put hours on brand new engines, or deliver an aircraft to a squadron, could end in tragedy when pilots took short cuts or were caught out by defective equipment or bad weather (figure 2).

To this day, the hills of Wales, the Peak District, the Lake District and Scotland are littered with the crash sites of flights which ended in tragedy. In southern Britain, the remains are more likely to have been those of machines engaged in combat. Kent, for example, is home to hundreds of aircraft crash sites from the second half of 1940, a time known as the Battle of Britain (10th July to 31st October 1940).

It was during the 1960s that a number of enthusiasts started to take an active interest in the physical remains of this era. Their excavations have provoked a lively debate and raised all sorts of interesting problems about archaeology and our heritage. There is no doubt that the air war of 1939–45 remains one of the most enthralling periods in modern

3. Spitfire V, BM597. This machine, built in 1942 at Castle Bromwich, has been restored and now flies at air displays. During the war it saw service with No. 315 Squadron from May 1942 to February 1943.

history, not only because of what was at stake but also because of the aircraft. We live in a remarkable age when the number of operational machines from the era is presently at an all-time high (since the war ended). The Supermarine Spitfire, without doubt the most famous aircraft of the war and arguably the most famous flying machine of all time, is now represented by around fifty flying examples (figures 3, 52), while many more reside in museums around the world. This interest has in part grown out of the excavation of relics from the war and at least one important British firm now engaged in reproducing components for flying Spitfires, Hurricanes, Messerschmitts and others has its origins directly in that activity.

Restorations allow us to appreciate these aviation artefacts in the medium for which they were designed. But aviation archaeology is unusual in its capacity to associate deeply buried physical remains with documented history. By its very nature, the recovery of artefacts cannot possibly recreate the spiritual background or the specific circumstances behind deposition. So conventional archaeologists are normally forced to recreate a general background to explain their sites. Divorced thus from the immediacy of human experience and the converging circumstances of an occasion, which includes the specific personalities involved, the archaeologist is handicapped from the start. These days, the recognition that unpredictable circumstances rather than just a set of background generalities must have been involved has allowed speculation about the effect of 'agencies'. This anodyne term at one stroke recognises that the world and its events are dictated by natural phenomena such as animals or people with all their various idiosyncrasies and also recognises that we normally cannot know who or what those were.

The vast majority of finds from wartime air-crash sites, and other pieces of evidence, are often rather uninspiring. Air crashes consist very largely of piles of scrap metal. Built for speed and lightness, a 1940s fighter aircraft was very strong when going in one direction (that is, forwards) and weak when going in any other. The trauma of impact normally wrecked the airframe, while fire could easily reduce much of the light alloy metal to powder. Where possible, the wreckage was removed at the time. A police report of 29th September 1940 states that the remains of Hurricane I, P3782, which crashed on 3rd September, were 'removed by an RAF Squad with a long, low, loader on Saturday the 26th September'. The evidence for this crash thus subsisted only in the contemporary documentation. It was not always evident even to the recovery teams at the time which machine they were recovering, and this has added to the confusion. In other cases, aircraft were left where they were, usually buried 2–4 metres (about 6–13 feet) below ground level. On hills, though, the wreckage was more likely to be distributed across the surface but terrain and remoteness still often meant it was abandoned (figure 4).

4. Wreckage of a 1944 United States Army Air Force P-47D Thunderbolt (42-75101) on a hill in North Wales as it is today. As with most remote crash sites, it was too difficult to remove the scattered fragments of airframe, now virtually unrecognisable as an aircraft (see figure 29). This machine crashed on a training flight from Atcham, Shropshire.

There is a great deal more to the remains of the air war than just the wreckage of aircraft. Britain became an 'island aircraft carrier' and even a casual glance at an Ordnance Survey map today reveals dozens of derelict airfields across the countryside. In a small number of cases, for example Thorpe Abbotts in Norfolk, enthusiasts have preserved some of the infrastructure in the form of a museum while elsewhere traces of runways and memorials add to the record. Paradoxically, the airfields are usually devoid of any obvious remnants of the aircraft. Crashed or scrapped, they generally lie elsewhere if they survive at all. Although many British crash sites are mentioned in this book, the fact is that the archaeological deposits of aircraft based in Britain spread right across Europe. Lancaster III, ND689, of No. 44 Squadron (then based at Dunholme, Lincolnshire) crashed on the night of 19th/20th May 1944 in a swamp in northern France at Long, near Amiens. Three of the engines were not located and recovered until the 1990s. One American B-17 Flying Fortress called *Skipper an' the Kids* flew a series of combat missions out of Knettishall, Norfolk, during 1944 but met its end on a navigational training exercise in Arran in December of that year (figure 34). Another American bomber, a B-24 Liberator (42-95095), had served with the 93rd Bombardment Group in Norfolk at Hardwick. With the European war over, a crew was allocated to fly it home to the United States but it crashed en route in the Fairy Lochs near Gairloch in north-west Scotland in June 1945.

Perhaps recovering or excavating the remains of these machines is a pointless activity. After all, we often know a great deal about the incidents because they are generally well recorded, or so it might be assumed. That is often not the case at all. Records are often incomplete, and local memories muddled. When the research is done and the remains recovered and removed to a museum, another episode in human history returns to the public domain (figure 5). This is, after all, part of what archaeology and history are all about. Both provide us with the means to reach out to the past and to touch and sense it.

The potency of the air war lies in its intoxicating mix of horror and bravery, as human beings were pushed to the very limits of their endurance during a conflict still affecting all our lives. This is no less valid a reason than the more self-conscious efforts by 'conventional' archaeologists to justify their activities. The present author has witnessed a number of 'normal' excavations but none was as compelling an experience as the recovery of a Spitfire in the company of the pilot's brother and one of his colleagues who had been there on that fateful day in 1940. Instead of just silent artefacts we learned about the life of one man and how the chaos of one day led to his death (figure 6). In the vast arid plain of archaeological anonymity the relics of the air war stand out

5. Airframe wreckage from Hurricane I, P2680, of No. 607 Squadron (Tangmere). Crashed at Stilstead Farm, East Peckham, Kent, on 9th September 1940, flown by Sergeant R. A. Spyer. Steel tubes made up the frame, stressed by bracing wires, each end of which was threaded for tightening to the correct tension.

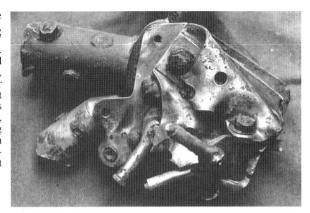

as monuments to an extraordinary period in our history. It is one which does not fail to move and fascinate visitors to the museums which have sprung up across Britain to house the relics of those who fell to earth in the last great war.

6. Despite being pulverised in a high-speed vertical impact on 23rd May 1940, parts of the airframe from Spitfire I, P9373, remain recognisable and evocative. These are the foot pedals, bearing the name Supermarine, manufacturers of this famous aircraft.

2
Documents and memorabilia

Throughout this book there are references to various sources of documentary information relating to the air war. They provide a vital resource. Anyone investigating air crashes and wreckage can find clues to locating sites this way, and once a site has been dug these sources will help identify the artefacts as well.

Having said that, the record is remarkably variable in its quality. Royal Air Force aircraft were provided with an individual record card, copies of which are now available through the archives stored at the RAF Museum, Hendon. In the early part of the war the information entered on it was usually fairly comprehensive and included the squadrons to which the machine had been allocated, and the dates. By late 1940 engine numbers were no longer routinely recorded, and there are blocks of aircraft for which the record cards are no longer extant. The records held by the Rolls-Royce Heritage Trust depend on private records made by an employee, the original records for each engine largely being destroyed after the war. Where an aircraft crashed in an accident, an Air Ministry Form 1180 (Accident Record Card) may be available. This will provide the machine's serial number, those of the engine(s), the location of the crash and the conditions which caused it.

Each unit had to provide an official record of its daily activities. For the RAF this is known as the Operational Record Book (Form F540) and is available for each squadron through the Public Record Office in Kew. Together with individual combat reports filed by pilots, and even unofficial diaries kept by individual squadrons, this source of information makes it possible (usually) to find out what had happened to an aircraft.

Pilots were obliged to keep their own logbooks, and these sometimes provide extraordinary detail for individual days and the usage of individual machines. An entry in the logbook of Flight Lieutenant J. M. Bazin, of No. 607 Squadron, reveals that on 11th September 1940 he flew Hurricane I, P2617, in combat. The aircraft survives at the RAF Museum, Hendon, but none of its official documentation testifies to an authentic Battle of Britain pedigree. Unfortunately, there is no means of verifying the information. Naturally enough, logbooks often remain with the pilots or their families. Those disposed of are often sold at auction, along with other effects like medals. Some are purchased by, or bequeathed to, institutions but an exceptional case is the logbook of Robert Stanford-Tuck who served with Spitfire and Hurricane squadrons in the Battle of Britain. This was bought by the *After the Battle* organisation, which has issued a facsimile of the logbook, effectively

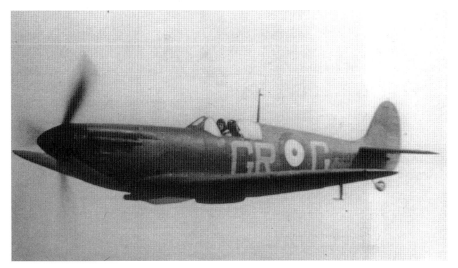

7. Spitfire I, P9372, GR-G, of No. 92 Squadron. Until private records emerged, this photograph taken in spring 1940 was the closest piece of evidence for identifying the squadron codes worn by the excavated Spitfire I, P9373, now known to have been GR-H (see figures 15, 16). (See chapter 5.) Later in the war the code was changed to 'QJ' (figure 37).

placing its contents in the public domain.

There is no better illustration of the sheer randomness of the record than the case of Spitfire I, P9373 (figures 6, 7). Despite the excavation of this machine and all the official documentation researched, it proved impossible to ascertain the aircraft's letter code which appeared on the fuselage. Daily records kept by the squadron (now available at the Public Record Office, Kew), the RAF and pilots made no mention of it. However, a book recently published about Croydon aerodrome includes the notes made by a schoolboy, G. A. Pott, in 1940. Pott noted that 'P9373 Spitfire I GR-H' took off at 1547 hours, returning at 1640 hours, on 30th March 1940. Amazingly, it proved possible to establish the notes were accurate through another reference to 'GR-S' taking off on the same day at 1529 hours. This was Allan Wright's Spitfire, N3250, and he made his logbook available to the author, which confirmed the time and date of his flight.

Records of American aircraft and units are maintained at the United States Air Force Historical Research Agency, Maxwell Air Force Base, Montgomery, Alabama. However, the Internet has so far proved considerably more useful to American veterans and many of their bombardment and fighter groups have individual websites. The present author found photographs taken by the 449th Bombardment Group,

8. The bombardment of Vienna in 1944. A photograph taken from a B-24 Liberator of the 449th Bombardment Group of the US Fifteenth Air Force, but found in a second-hand bookshop in Kent.

based in southern Italy in 1944–5, in a Kent bookshop. The Internet turned up a site devoted to the unit which also carried details of all the raids conducted by the group, allowing some of the photographs to be identified (figure 8).

The find is typical of discoveries in a myriad of junk-shops around Britain where all sorts of obscure remnants of the air war can be chanced upon. An old radio labelled 'army radio' turned up in an all-purpose junk-shop in south-east London. On closer examination it turned out to be marked 'AM' for Air Ministry and was an R1155B model, a type of radio receiver fitted to British bombers and fighter-bombers. Inside it bears stamps recording its wartime maintenance by the RAF. Perhaps most extraordinarily it was in working order, having been modified in the early 1950s, according to documents accompanying it. Although it will never be possible to identify which aircraft it was operated in, there can be

9. British R1155 receiver. This type of radio was a standard fitment to British bombers in the Second World War. This example was disposed of as war surplus and by the early 1950s it had been modified for domestic use. It was found by the author in a Greenwich junk shop in 1997 and was in complete working order.

10. Soldiers carry away a tail fin from Messerschmitt Bf 110C-4 ('Werke' no. 3113) of I/ZG2 which crashed at Pudsey Hall Farm, Canewdon, Essex, on 3rd September 1940. The swastika was later cut from the relic and turned up in an Army & Navy window display from where it entered the collections of *After the Battle* magazine.

no doubt that it survives as a functioning component of the air war, which will help identify shattered parts excavated from sites (figure 9).

Finding souvenirs taken from crashes during the war can also lead to relocating forgotten crash sites. A Messerchmitt Bf 110 crashed at Pudsey Hall Farm, Canewdon, Essex, on 3rd September 1940. Clearance of the wreckage was photographed for British propaganda purposes (figure 10). Many years later, the swastika on the tail was discovered in a shop display; it must have been cut from the fin around the time of the crash. Unlabelled, it would have been unidentifiable were it not for the photograph and it has now entered the collection of *After the Battle* magazine.

The photographic archive of the air war is an exceptional but erratic resource, like the rest of the record. Many incidents were never recorded. Some squadrons were well photographed by enthusiastic individuals, or as a result of visits by professional units, while others are practically absent from the record. *After the Battle* publications are highly recommended because a concerted effort has been made to identify places and events in the photographs, which, because of the wartime need to suppress exact information, were frequently left unlabelled. Photographs of the same places or people were then taken many years later and the two published together in a magnificent series of books and magazines that has done a tremendous amount to put on record for all time material which might otherwise have been overlooked. It is also the case that certain units, such as the US Eighth Air Force, are generally

11. The remains of Dornier Do 17Z-2 of 9/KG 76 near Leaves Green, Kent, after the battle of 18th August 1940. Damaged by anti-aircraft fire from Kenley during the raid, it was finished off by Hurricanes of No. 111 Squadron. A panel bearing the swastika survives today in the RAF Museum at Hendon.

well served by books while other units, such as the US Ninth Air Force (also based in Britain), scarcely feature at all.

Crashed enemy aircraft were a favourite subject for propaganda press photographs though the precise location was often suppressed (figure 11). Nevertheless, trees and skylines make identification possible so long as building and road construction have not irremediably altered the landscape.

Of course, documents, memorabilia and photographs are no substitute for fieldwork. Locating a crash site is a skilled business. It involves tracing skylines from photographs, if available, and then laboriously exploring the land for surface fragments of airframe and engines, and perhaps even visible cratering. It may turn out that a once open site is now built over and inaccessible, or that trees have grown up in what was once grassland. Some crashes, particularly those on high ground, remained on the surface but many others became deeply buried in soil or marshland. From a technical point of view this can make location and excavation substantially more difficult than in conventional archaeology, where deposits are rarely as deep (figure 12).

Identifying components from wrecked aircraft can be something of a challenge (see chapter 5). A few components are obvious, such as the propeller or control handle. But fragments of piping, hydraulics, airframe sections and shattered pieces of engine casing can prove a problem. Despite the popularity of the period and the attendant research, it is very hard to locate manuals, blueprints and parts lists, and it usually proves necessary to borrow copies and photocopy them.

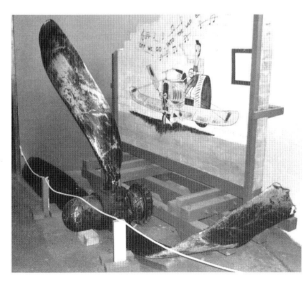

12. Propeller from a 385th Bombardment Group B-17G Flying Fortress (42-31370), displayed in the museum at Thorpe Abbotts, Norfolk. Extracting this unit from the marsh at Reedham (Norfolk) in 1978 involved years of planning, considerable expense and difficulty in digging into the swampy ground. Other items from the same machine were not recovered for more than twenty years (see front cover and figure 17).

3
Excavations

Regardless of how a crash site has been identified, aviation archaeology remains controversial and fraught with practical and legal problems. Crashed British military aircraft are legally the property of the government, which means the Ministry of Defence. It makes no difference where the machine's remains are, or whether they are lying on the surface or underground. Crashed enemy aircraft are regarded as 'spoils' of war and are treated the same. American aircraft are technically the property of the United States government but in practice the British government deals with them. Different conditions apply to British and American aircraft which crashed on the mainland of Europe, but in many cases the legal restrictions are more relaxed.

There are sound reasons for all these controls. Military aircraft are liable to have been carrying bombs and bullets. Astonishingly durable, these are extremely dangerous (figure 13). There is also the question of human remains, provoking a conflict of interests. The official approach is normally to prevent excavations of machines believed to contain human remains. General public opinion normally supports that point of view. But often the families of air crew find the absence of a known grave unsettling and wish to see their relative recovered and buried

13. Following the excavation of a B-17G Flying Fortress near Reedham, Norfolk, unfired bullets were removed by members of the RAF. They were buried in a shallow pit and blown up in a controlled explosion – the only safe way to dispose of munitions.

14. Propeller blade from a Heinkel He 111 (note the contemporary misspelling). The inscription identifies it as a machine which crashed at Burgess Farm, Frittenden, Kent, on 15th September 1940. This machine is known from other records to have been no. 6843 of II/KG53, shot down at 4.00 p.m. that day.

properly. The excavation of Flight Lieutenant Hugh Beresford's Hurricane I, P3049, in 1979 is a particularly good example. Beresford was with No. 257 Squadron in the autumn of 1940 when he was shot down and killed on 7th September. His aircraft crashed into swampy ground on the Isle of Sheppey in the Thames estuary, probably accounting for why his body was not recovered during the war. The excavation in 1979 was not only filmed for television but was welcomed by Beresford's sister, who then participated in her brother's full military funeral at Brookwood Military Cemetery.

Beresford's case also illustrates the practical problems of organising an excavation. Any aviation group that wishes to excavate an aircraft has first to locate a site. This means using a combination of eyewitness accounts (which are becoming much rarer), police records and official RAF records as described in the previous chapter. Even souvenirs taken at the time may bear labels with useful information (figure 14). The official accident report form for Spitfire IX, NH523, tells us that it crashed on 20th January 1945 when the pilot lost control in cloud as well as stating the crash site to be 'Stanton Wyville, 5 miles N[orth] M[arket] Harborough'.

Field-walking then follows to try to locate the crash site from fragments of metal scattered on the surface, or perhaps by a visible dip in a field. Of course, field-walking itself can sometimes expose a crash before its identity is known. A Spitfire I was excavated near Boulogne having been identified first from local information and the pilot's grave in the churchyard; it was located by field-walking, which happened to yield a fragment from an ammunition feed chute bearing its serial number

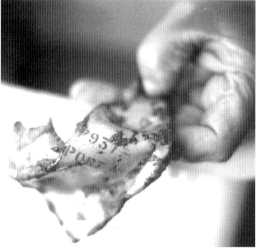

15. Fragment of ammunition feed bearing the stencilled serial number P9373 identifying the remains as a Spitfire of No. 92 Squadron shot down on 23rd May 1940 over Wierre-Effroy near Boulogne. (See also figures 6, 7, 16 and 18).

(figure 15), an unusually fortunate development. Conventional archaeological surface-scraping revealed its entry hole (figure 16), any cratering having long since been wiped out by agriculture.

Once an accessible site has been located and a possible identity established, the next stage is to see whether the site is likely to be a war

16. The entry hole of Spitfire I, P9373, is clearly visible in the cleaned and scraped surface. The discolouration is caused by disturbance, different moisture content and contamination from aviation fuel and lubricating oil released as the engine exploded (see also figures 6, 7, 15 and 18).

grave; permission to excavate (in the form of a Ministry of Defence licence) is unlikely to be awarded in such cases. If there is no reason to suspect a body at the site and the group can present themselves as *bona fide* enthusiasts a licence to dig may be granted. Even so, permission from the landowner is essential as well and, considering the nature of aviation excavations, may not be forthcoming.

Digging up aeroplanes is not for the faint-hearted. Engines and propellers are extremely heavy and often buried up to 5 metres (at least 16 feet) or more below the surface. This means bringing heavy plant on to the site (figure 17). The difficulty of recovery was very often the reason why engines and other heavy components were left where they were or even reburied at the time. A pair of B-17G Flying Fortress bombers of the 385th Bombardment Group collided over Reedham Marsh, Norfolk, on 21st February 1944. Both aircraft were destroyed and both crews killed. It took a considerable amount of footwork on the part of local enthusiasts to identify the scattered wreckage but the research uncovered contemporary photos of a United States Army Air Force recovery crew engaged in removing what they could, and this had included all the bodies. However, one of the aircraft had crashed sufficiently far into the marsh to make it unlikely that any heavy components had been recovered.

17. Excavating an engine from the B-17G Flying Fortress (42-31370) of the 385th Bombardment Group in Norfolk marshland at Reedham involved a great deal of arduous and frustrating work to dig a deep and safe hole.

This site was a good example of where there was likely to be something left, but the main reason wreckage was still there was the difficult access. Marshland, typical of many parts of coastal south and eastern England, is very difficult to excavate: the ground cannot support heavy plant, and any deep excavation will fill with water quickly. At Reedham metal-detectors had indicated the presence of major components. Planning then meant providing timber to act as a surface for caterpillar tracks and pumps to keep the hole dry (figure 17). But marshland is also liable to move unpredictably and quickly, leading to unexpected slippage of the sides of an excavated trench, quite apart from environmental considerations. All this needed to be organised and, as this was a bomber, preparations had to be made for dealing with bombs. Under such conditions it is fairly obvious that traditional archaeological techniques of gentle trowelling and scraping would be inappropriate and possibly dangerous.

Spitfire II, P7386, crashed at Sandwich, Kent, on 14th November 1940. A private company was contracted to recover the wreckage on behalf of the RAF maintenance units (who at the time were overwhelmed by the crashes which needed clearing). The engine was located at a depth of 6 metres (20 feet). Despite using heavy plant over several days, the job was abandoned and the engine is still there.

One of the great problems with excavating aircraft is unstable metal. In the 1930s and 1940s magnesium alloys were heavily relied on for their lightness, a vital property for airframes. Unfortunately magnesium decomposes very easily and components made from it rarely survive. The magnesium often disintegrates into a flaky grey powder. For this reason Spitfire wheels and control handles (figure 18), as well as other components, are virtually never recovered from excavations. A B-17 engine from the Reedham site was in advanced decay, even more obvious on a different engine recovered from the sea (see front cover, and figure 19).

More straightforward are crash sites where the wreckage lies on the surface, but all the legal considerations are equally applicable (figure 4). A variant on this is where aircraft are lying underwater. Land crashes normally involved comprehensive destruction of the wings and much of the airframe. A Messerschmitt Bf 109E-4 (4853) of 2/JG51 was shot down off Dymchurch, Kent, on 7th October 1940. The pilot was rescued but the aircraft sank and was located by a fisherman in 1974. Much of the aircraft was recovered by the Brenzett Museum group, though it was not until the metal had been stabilised and examined that its identity could be established. The identity of a Halifax which ended up at the bottom of a Norwegian lake was already known and it was recovered in remarkable condition (figures 20, 26).

The work done by wartime recovery crews should not be overlooked.

18. The firing button from Spitfire I, P9373, shot down on 23rd May 1940 in France. The magnesium spade-handle grip has rotted away completely, leaving only the brass button fitting.

With so much wreckage to dispose of, there was considerable convenience in simply burying it. Spitfire V, AD540, crashed at Carsphairn, Kirkcudbrightshire, in unknown circumstances on 23rd May 1942. Named *Blue Peter* by a contemporary group who had contributed to its cost, it came to wider notice when the producers of the popular children's television programme of the same name were told about it.

19. Pratt & Whitney twin-row Wasp radial engine, with three-bladed propeller, noted in a Kent scrapyard. Recovered from the sea, from an unknown aircraft of the Second World War (probably a B-24 Liberator or Douglas C-47 Skytrain), it is in an extremely advanced state of decomposition.

20. A restored Merlin engine from Halifax II, W1048 (see figure 26). The view is the rear right-hand side and shows the supercharger assembly (left) and starter motor gear (centre).

Once it was learned that the machine had crashed in the war they determined to locate it. It emerged that the wreckage had been gathered and deliberately buried on a lonely hillside. Finding it proved extremely difficult, though, once located, uncovering it was fairly easy. Even so, only the use of an RAF helicopter made its removal possible.

Many aircraft are now completely inaccessible. This is because they are either too deeply buried, or now covered by buildings, or even because they crashed through structures remaining largely intact. Sergeant Ray Holmes shot down a Dornier bomber over Victoria station in London on 15th September 1940 but was forced to bale out himself. His Hurricane I, P2725, is still below the surface of Buckingham Palace Road in London and is likely to stay there indefinitely, though fragments gathered at the time were presented to Winston Churchill and remain in his estate. The circumstances have defied every attempt to organise a recovery of some historical significance: the events of that day were captured on film and have remained one of the most powerful images of the Battle of Britain.

4
Engines and airframes

The engine is the heaviest and most durable component of an aircraft of the Second World War and dominates site finds or, at any rate, those finds which have been recovered. Fighters normally had one, though some had two, and bombers tended to have two or four. Single-engine aircraft invariably have the motor located in the fuselage but in almost all other cases the engines were installed in the wings. Regardless of the different designs and configurations, most engines were equipped with superchargers. The supercharger is a sealed-fan device which elevates the pressure of the air being sucked in by the engine to compensate for thin air at high altitude and thereby keep the engine running efficiently high above the ground. It also allows the pressure to be increased above sea level to boost power even higher. An ingenious device, it was absolutely essential in combat or for bombers like the B-17 which relied on high altitude for safety.

In crashes the engine(s) normally broke free, either during the fall or as the aircraft exploded on impact. The engine rarely remained intact, though it was common for the main block to remain in one large piece with peripherals such as the supercharger and carburettor (if fitted) scattered nearby.

Despite the large number of different types of aircraft used, the range of piston engines was limited to a few basic models but with many variations. This 'power egg' concept meant that the same engine can be found on several different aircraft, and deposits, and that an individual engine may have been used on several different aircraft in its lifetime.

Engines can be initially divided into two types: air-cooled and liquid-cooled. Air-cooled engines are normally 'radial' in layout. This means that the cylinders (usually nine) are arranged around the central crankshaft, thereby resembling a starfish. This presents a large face to the slipstream to maximise air-flow around the cylinders, which also had multiple fins (similar to a motorcycle engine). These increased the surface area from which heat could be dispersed. Power could be increased by adding another row of nine cylinders behind.

Radial engines were fairly simple, but solid. The design was 'older', but it remained popular throughout the war with aircraft like the German Dornier Do17, the American B-17 Flying Fortress and B-24 Liberator, and the British Handley-Page Halifax all making use of them. The principal advantage was durability because they could suffer considerable damage while continuing to work. The main disadvantage was the drag they produced by presenting a large face to the slipstream (front cover and figure 19).

21. The Rolls-Royce Merlin III engine. The design is a twelve-cylinder, in a V-configuration of two banks of six, liquid-cooled motor weighing 1375 pounds (624 kg), capable of producing 1030 horsepower. Comparisons are difficult, but the power generated is around ten times that of an average 2 litre car or today's light training aeroplanes. By the end of the war the Merlin had been so improved that its power had been almost doubled. The engine is also equipped with a supercharger, a sealed fan-and-vane device making good the reduction in air pressure at altitude by forcing air through narrow cavities at ultra-high speed. (Courtesy of Rolls-Royce Heritage Trust.)

Liquid-cooled engines resolved this, by allowing banks of cylinders to be arranged 'in line' (figure 21). The liquid-cooling made good the lack of air-cooling and also maintained a more stable temperature, which made for more consistent and greater performance. Unfortunately, the engines were very susceptible to damage. A blown cooling system could cause rapid overheating and lead to the pilot baling out, half-blinded by the escaping cooling liquid in vapour form. This was one of the commonest causes of abandoning an otherwise undamaged aircraft.

The Rolls-Royce Merlin

The Merlin engine, the most famous of all aero-engines, was developed in the 1930s. Two rows of six liquid-cooled cylinders arranged in a V-configuration drove a common crankshaft. This V-12 assembly included a substantial gear and propeller shaft at the front, and at the other end a carburettor and a supercharger (figure 21).

The Merlin was not the only example of this kind of engine, but it was the most successful. Amongst its numerous variants was the American-built Packard used in the P-51 Mustang, and which was also installed in some British aircraft such as the Lancaster III and the Spitfire XVI. At the beginning of the war, the Merlin was at an early stage of development. Spitfires and Hurricanes in the Battle of Britain made use of the 1030 horsepower Merlin III. By the end of the war the design had been retained but higher octane fuel, improved carburation and supercharging in versions like the Merlin 65 had raised the power output to over 1700 horsepower.

The basic structure of the Merlin was a series of aluminium-alloy cast casings. During assembly the heavy internals, such as the crankshaft, connecting rods, pistons, valves and camshafts were all installed and then the cases bolted down. Ancillary components like starting gear (either an electric motor, or cartridge firing unit), water-pumps and piping were added to create the finished unit.

The Merlin engine looks extremely solid. In a crash it was anything but, and even in ordinary service its casing was prone to cracking. The alloy was extremely brittle, while in crashes metal propeller blades

22. Rolls-Royce Merlin III engine fitted to Hurricane I, P3115, of No. 253 Squadron which crashed at Cudham, Kent, on 31st August 1940 while being piloted by Squadron Leader T. P. Gleave. Gleave survived, having baled out, but was badly burned. Remarkably, the engine lay in woodland for decades before recovery. However, as normal, the supercharger/carburettor assembly and reduction gear assembly (compare with figure 21) had been blown off in the impact. Now displayed at Duxford.

caused a good deal of resistance, forcing the engine, then turning over at more than 3000 rpm, to stop abruptly. The substantial internal steel parts like the crankshaft were liable at that moment to erupt and tear through the casings. Pistons were likely to seize in their cylinders and the immense force created by this could cause them to tear away from the crankshaft. The propeller shaft and gear broke up and away. The casings of the supercharger and carburettor were considerably thinner and these broke up into small pieces very quickly (figure 22).

All this happened as the aircraft wreckage drove into the ground. The nature of the soil and the angle of the crash could both greatly affect the engine's fate. Stony soil offers greater resistance and causes greater damage than soft soil or sand. Hurricane I, P3815, flown by Sergeant F. J. Kozlowski of No. 501 Squadron, crashed near Whitstable, Kent, on 18th August 1940. Although the main core of the engine was found to be intact, the propeller gear and the front of the engine had been torn off, and the entire supercharger/carburettor assembly on the back had also been ripped away exposing the starter and coolant-pump drive gears (figure 23).

23. Shattered wheelcase (gearbox) from the Merlin III fitted to Hurricane I, P3815, flown by Sergeant F. J. Kozlowski of No. 501 Squadron on 18th August 1940. The aircraft crashed near Whitstable, Kent. Kozlowski survived, injured, but was killed in 1943. The visible devices are: generator drive (far left), magneto drives (top centre), supercharger drive (centre), fuel pump drive (bottom centre) and starter transmission (far right). The actual starter would fill the void at lower right but, along with the complete supercharger and carburettor, has broken away entirely. Now displayed at Manston museum.

24. The remains of Hurricane I, P3175, DT-S. Delivered to No. 257 Squadron (Debden) on 9th August 1940, it crashed on 31st August 1940, killing Pilot Officer G. H. Maffett. The remains were excavated from coastal marshes at Walton-on-the-Naze, Essex. This is the only excavated example of a Battle of Britain aircraft displayed in a national collection. The wooden propeller blades have snapped off, allowing the engine to slow down without self-destructing.

The damage to Kozlowski's machine was typical but Pilot Officer G. H. Maffett's Hurricane I, P3175, of No. 257 Squadron, crashed into the sand at Walton-on-the-Naze, Essex, on 31st August 1940. Maffett was killed but the front part of his aircraft sank steadily into the sand, where it lay until it was excavated in the 1970s. It now resides in the RAF Museum at Hendon (figure 24). Unusually, the engine is almost entirely intact, together with the propeller boss and all other peripherals, as well as having stayed with the airframe. The broken wooden propeller blades are part of the reason. By shattering on impact they allowed the engine to slow down of its own accord, and not self-destruct. Careful and thoughtful excavation here allowed the entire assemblage to be recovered and it remains the only excavated fighter of the era to be exhibited in a national museum.

The high-speed impact of Spitfire I, P9373, on 23rd May 1940 could not have been more different. Although the engine remained with the airframe the aircraft entered stony farmland in a vertical dive. The force

25. Oil-filter mount from a Merlin III engine sump fitted to Spitfire I, R6753, XT-G, flown by Pilot Officer D. J. C. Pinckney. Pinckney flew with No. 603 Squadron and was a personal friend of Richard Hillary, who found him dangling from his parachute in a tree after both had been shot down on 29th August 1940 (*The Last Enemy*, pages 133–4). The bolts have been swept back by the force of the crash, which then tore this component from the engine body. Diameter 135 mm.

was so great that the wreckage was compressed. At least one of the metal propeller blades survived the initial impact and it caused the engine to stop abruptly, at which point the Merlin exploded. On excavation this was testified to by the fact that seven of the twelve cylinders had torn off and burst through the cylinder walls. The parallel cylinder heads had become twisted round each other. The entire crankcase had been smashed into hundreds of fragments. On one hand the twisted and wrecked components are a powerful image of the dynamic of an air crash. On the other they illustrate the extreme difficulty of excavating fragmented wreckage. Re-excavation of other machines, more hastily dug, can reveal large engine components overlooked during the initial dig (figure 25).

Not all aircraft crash at high speed. Halifax II, W1048, force-landed on the frozen surface of Lake Höklingen in Norway on 27th April 1942. It had been damaged during an attack on the German battleship *Tirpitz*. The crew abandoned her but an engine fire gradually melted the ice and the aircraft sank to the bottom. Recovered for display at Hendon, the remains nevertheless still show the tendency for the heavy engines to break away from the airframe. The engines are intact and have even yielded serviceable components like starter motors, but each had snapped away under its weight (figures 20, 26). The machine is also a reminder that British aviation archaeology can range far beyond the shores of Britain itself.

Radial engines

Radial engines can be compared to a solid barrel containing the gears and crankshaft, with the cylinders radiating around. This central core seems to have had a reasonably high chance of survival in crashes.

26. Handley-Page Halifax II, W1048, in the condition it was found at the bottom of Lake Höklingen in Norway. It made a forced landing on the frozen lake surface on 27th April 1942 during an attack on the German battleship *Tirpitz*. It is the only original Halifax extant and is displayed at the RAF Museum, Hendon. Note how the weight of the port inner engine has caused it to snap free from the wing mount. This characteristic explains how engines often separated from the airframe because of the much greater forces of a crash from altitude (see also figure 20).

Relatively few fighters made use of them in Europe during the Second World War apart from the German Focke-Wulf Fw 190 and the American Thunderbolt. The most widely used were the Wright Cyclone nine-cylinder radial fitted to the B-17 Flying Fortress (front cover), and the Pratt & Whitney twin-row eighteen-cylinder Wasp fitted to, amongst others, the B-24 Liberator and P-47 Thunderbolt.

The degree of durability can easily be seen in a Thunderbolt crash on a Welsh hilltop in May 1944. Here the pilot seems to have attempted a forced landing, probably in mist and cloud. The aircraft was destroyed and the scattered wreckage subsisting to this day shows that the airframe was completely shattered on impact (figure 27). However, the Pratt & Whitney Wasp engine has survived very largely intact, though souvenir hunters have stripped the cylinder heads and some of the peripherals.

More tantalising is a similar engine noticed in a Kent scrapyard (figure 19). This engine survives along with its propeller, having been gathered from the sea. It is likely to have come from a B-24 Liberator or a Douglas C-47 Skytrain. Unfortunately, its history is now unrecoverable. But it shows that, while an engine could survive a crash in remarkably intact form, the nature of the metals used has allowed it to deteriorate steadily. The alloy cylinders are now disintegrating into the characteristic flaky grey powder. Such is its weakness that steel internals, like valve springs, have caused the surrounding alloy metal to crack.

Recovering a Wright Cyclone nine-cylinder radial from a B-17G Flying

27. Pratt & Whitney twin-row radial Wasp engine from P-47D Thunderbolt 42-75101, photographed in 1999 on Mynydd Copog near Bala in Wales, where it fell in 1944.

Fortress (42-31370) which crashed on 21st February 1944 was extremely successful (front cover). The aircraft crashed into a marsh, making it unlikely that the components would be substantially damaged. But documentary and photographic evidence from the period shows that the USAAF attended the crash site and removed very large quantities of wreckage from the surface. It was normal practice in difficult conditions to gather major parts like engines and bury them in pits on site, rather than attempt to move them away. It is quite possible that this engine's survival was largely due to this. Although it was found buried at a depth of more than 4 metres (over 13 feet), this was almost certainly due to gradual sinkage into the marshy soil. An interesting feature of this dig was that the anaerobic conditions of the marsh were such that aviation fuel, oil and organic materials such as rubber, leather and wood were well preserved but the unstable alloys used in the engine were already wreaking havoc. Much of the engine was steadily disintegrating.

Airframes

Aircraft fly because their engines pull them through the atmosphere fast enough to create lift over the wings. In section, the upper side of the wing is longer than the underside. As the aircraft moves through the atmosphere the air above the wing takes longer to pass over than the air underneath. The molecules in the air above become more widely dispersed and the pressure is reduced compared to the air underneath. The air below, having higher pressure, thus holds the aeroplane up.

A stationary aircraft has no lift. Only when air passes across the wing is the necessary pressure discrepancy produced. Anyone travelling in an airliner today will be aware that the aircraft has to accelerate down the runway until the moment when lift occurs and the machine takes off – rotates – into the air. Even if engines fail in flight, lift can be sustained by a gradual gliding descent.

In the twenty-first century aviation technology is so advanced that aircraft can be created on computers with the certainty that they will fly. In the early days of aviation the rules of flight were still being learned. Aircraft builders realised two things. First, they needed power plants which could pull their machines through the air and, secondly, they needed to make life as easy as possible for the engines by making the structure of the aircraft – the airframe – as light and as streamlined as possible.

Early aircraft were built almost entirely of wood and fabric. The relatively feeble engines of the day needed all the help they could get and therefore most aircraft were designed with two wings, one above the other. These are known as biplanes. Unfortunately the extra wing meant more drag, literally friction against the air, but, given the slow speeds of the aircraft, this was not an overwhelming problem.

During the 1920s and 1930s engine development proceeded apace, and so did the development of materials. Higher speeds, in excess of 480 km/h (300 mph), became possible and this produced new problems. Drag increases with speed, making biplanes not only undesirable but cumbersome. New aircraft had to be better streamlined, stronger but still light.

This led to the crop of new monoplane fighters such as the Messerschmitt Bf 109 and the Hawker Hurricane. Not surprisingly old techniques were mixed with the new. The Hurricane grew out of a stable of 1920s military biplanes, based on a wood-and-fabric airframe. The Hurricane's airframe depended on a braced-girder structure in which a metal and wood frame was tightened and stressed with steel wire. Despite being effective and strong in service a crash could pulverise the wreckage (figure 28). Where the ground was more yielding, the stronger areas (mainly the cockpit, engine mountings and wing spar) might remain moderately intact (figure 24), but this is exceptionally rare.

The Spitfire and other more 'modern' aircraft relied on a structure known as monocoque. The aircraft was built around a frame of light alloy struts and 'formers' (shaped panels which created the basic shape), all of which had as many holes and drillings as possible to reduce weight. The strength lay in the surface skinning made from accurately

28. Wreckage of Spitfire I, P9373, piloted by Sergeant Paul Klipsch of No. 92 Squadron uncovered in a field in France. The tailwheel can be seen in the centre while fragments of the engine lie at the bottom. The force of impact has compressed the complete fuselage into a stack little more than 1.5 metres (about 5 feet) high.

cut and shaped metal sheets (usually duralumin, or alclad) riveted into place. This is similar to how modern cars are built. The structure was immensely strong and flexible in flight but it was costly to repair and in a crash was liable to crumple out of recognition (figures 4, 28). Excavators are left with a large quantity of alloy and steel twisted into barely identifiable scrap which often defies restoration or display – hence the bias to engine displays in museums. Nevertheless, the force of impact often causes wings and tail units to smash into pieces on the surface. These were usually gathered up at the time by RAF clearance crews. Conversely, where fighters crashed, the engine was liable to pull much of the fuselage behind it underground, leaving the wings behind. Bombers were more likely to be scattered on the surface, as the engines would normally break away from the wings. The greater size of the fuselage offered more resistance to burial and there was no fuselage engine to drag it into the ground.

Paradoxically, one of the most successful aircraft of the entire period, the de Havilland Mosquito, reverted to wood for the airframe. A highly refined design made the most of the wood's lightness and advanced forms of the Merlin engine to produce one of the fastest fighter-bombers of the war. Inevitably, physical remains of these aircraft at crash sites are almost entirely confined to the engines, undercarriage and fittings.

5
Identifications

A crashed aircraft, whether on the surface or underground, is usually an almost unrecognisable heap of scrap, regardless of how carefully it has been excavated. But the purpose behind the dig is usually to confirm its identity, based on the documentary or other evidence which drew attention to the crash in the first place.

While it may be possible with care and knowledge to identify major parts, and thus the model or type involved, being sure which aircraft is involved may be a much more difficult task. Even identifying the type may be far from easy. Features regarded as diagnostic, such as the Spitfire's elliptical wings, are easily destroyed in high-speed impacts. Not only that, but military aircraft, unlike cars, do not proudly display manufacturer's and model names.

So, it is left to the surviving components to provide the answers. But this is not straightforward either. The engine is likely to be the most recognisable part. The Rolls-Royce Merlin III engine, for example, was used in all the front-line fighters in the Battle of Britain: Spitfire, Hurricane and Defiant. Finding a crash site with the remains of one of these engines, or even individual components, does not identify the aircraft. The Merlin engine went through a series of developments through the war. For example, the Merlin XX engine was used in the Lancaster I, the Hurricane II and the Beaufighter II. However, some of the same components were used in different versions. Merlin part numbers are preceded by the letter 'D'. Pistons marked D10952 are, for example, found in Merlin III and XX engines as well as other models. Similar considerations apply to German and American aircraft. The Jumo 211 engine, for example, was used in the Junkers Ju 87 and Ju 88 machines.

However, all aircraft of the Second World War carried their own individual serial numbers. This was the number allocated by the RAF, the USAAF or the *Luftwaffe*. In the RAF's case, the serial consisted of a letter and four digits, or two letters and three digits. That number was used on the aircraft's record card, and it was also the number used in squadron archives. The number was stencilled on either side of the rear fuselage though it was sometimes partially obscured by squadron code letters or camouflage. An internal manufacturer's plate might carry it too.

American aircraft had longer serial numbers, usually painted on the tail and also stencilled on to some internal components. The number always began with a 4, thus 42-37963 was a B-17G Flying Fortress of

29. Republic P-47 Thunderbolt (42-25234 as 42-8487), similar to the crashed machine in figures 4 and 27. It bears the markings of the 56th Fighter Group of the US Eighth Air Force, based in Britain from late 1942 to 1945, but now flies from Chino, California, where this picture was taken. The lower engine cowlings have been removed for servicing.

the 385th Bombardment Group which crashed into Reedham Marsh in Norfolk on 21st February 1944. An abbreviated, but prominent, form of the serial number appeared on the aircraft fin, in this case '237963' (compare with figure 31), but the complete form together with model details was painted on the front left fuselage below the pilot's window. *Luftwaffe* aircraft had a four-digit *Werke* number which was usually painted on the tail.

The aircraft kept the number throughout its life and when it was destroyed or scrapped the number went with it and was never used again. In an excavation, finding a component with this individual serial

30. Fragment of airframe bearing the numbers [V]6638. This identifies the associated wreckage as Hurricane I, V6638, of No. 253 Squadron piloted by Flying Officer A. A. G. Trueman and lost over Banstead, Surrey, on 4th September 1940. Photographed by courtesy of Colin Lee.

31. The B-17G *Sally B*, which carries the squadron markings and serial number of the celebrated 91st Bombardment Group B-17F *Memphis Belle*. The real *Memphis Belle* survives in Memphis, Tennessee, but this machine was built in the spring of 1945 and is now based at Duxford, Cambridgeshire.

number is the only way to make a firm identification of the wreckage and tie it up with official records. Fortunately, the serial number was often stencilled on to internal parts to aid re-assembly after major repairs or servicing. V6638 was the serial number of a Hurricane I of No. 253 Squadron, based at Kenley, Surrey. It crashed on 4th September 1940 in Banstead, Surrey, killing the pilot, Flying Officer A. A. G. Trueman. The crash site was not located until long afterwards but was confirmed by a small piece of airframe with the serial number stamped on it (figure 30). Spitfire I, P9373, of No. 92 (East India) Squadron, which crashed in Wierre-Effroy in France on 23rd May 1940, while being flown from Hornchurch, Essex, by Sergeant Paul Klipsch, was positively identified from a piece of a machine-gun ammunition feed collected while field-walking (figure 15).

Unfortunately, this kind of evidence is unusual. Nevertheless, crashed aircraft are packed with other components carrying numbers and letters. Each may provide a vital clue by identifying the country of origin, manufacturer and perhaps the type. Parts bearing a crown and the letters AM refer to the British Air Ministry (figure 32). Equally, a radio part with the legend 'Signal Corps, US Army' speaks for itself. These help, but some parts made in America were used in British machines, like the Packard version of the Rolls-Royce Merlin. Fragments of one of these could come from an American P-51 Mustang or a British Lancaster, as well as a Spitfire XVI.

32. This brass T-connector is stamped AM for Air Ministry, thus marking it as being from a British aircraft. It is part of the oxygen feed system from Spitfire I, X4276, of No. 54 Squadron, which crashed after a mid-air collision with another Spitfire from the same squadron on 29th December 1940 while being piloted by the then Flight Lieutenant Alan Deere DFC.

Some airframe components carry numbers and codes helping to identify the model. For example, serials beginning '300...' refer to the Spitfire Mark I. This was the Vickers-Supermarine factory code for the model (figure 33). German aircraft are sometimes more helpful in this respect, with certain components carrying parts numbers which include the model number: Thus an alloy casting from the undercarriage, which includes '111' as a distinct part of the number, shows that it is from a Heinkel He 111. Conversely, a plate from a B-17G specifies the model unequivocally (figure 34).

If engines are not automatically definitive, they can contribute information. Most carry some sort of identifying plate (figure 35). Even

33. Section of Spitfire airframe former, bearing the serial number 300... denoting a Spitfire I. From the wreckage of L1067 XT-D of No. 603 Squadron, flown by Squadron Leader G. L. Denholm on 30th August 1940. Crashed at Snargate, Kent.

34. Manufacturer's plate identifying associated wreckage as a B-17G Flying Fortress. From the crash site of *Skipper an' the Kids*, a US Eighth Air Force B-17G (42-97286) of the 388th Bombardment Group based at Knettishall, which struck high ground on the Island of Arran on 10th December 1944. While the plate does not specify the aircraft concerned, the type is confirmed and this provides a vital initial clue. Photographed by courtesy of Colin Lee.

without this, the components can yield surprises. The Rolls-Royce Merlin, for example, carried a serial number for the whole unit, stamped into various locations on the engine. This Rolls-Royce number was recorded alongside an Air Ministry number for the same engine in official records. Spitfire PR.IV (a photo-reconnaissance model), AB130, crashed in 1942, and its Merlin engine has since been recovered. The RAF crash report for this machine records the Air Ministry number for the engine, AM 280854. When Rolls-Royce records were consulted this Air Ministry number was matched by the Rolls-Royce number M

35. Jumo 211 engine plate said to be from the Junkers Ju 88A-5 (*Werke* no. 0293) shot down by fighters and anti-aircraft fire at Vexour Farm, Penshurst, Kent.

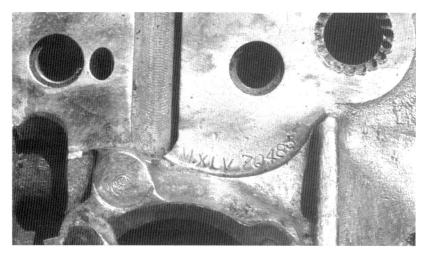

36. Cylinder head from Spitfire PR.IV, AB130, of No. 140 Squadron, which crashed on 26th August 1942. The engine number, M XLV 70483 (= Merlin 45, no. 70483), can be tied up in Rolls-Royce records to the Air Ministry number AM280854, the number recorded on the crash report for this Spitfire, thus confirming its identity.

XLV (= Merlin type 45) 70483, the very serial number which is visible on the engine parts today (figure 36). This confirms the aircraft's identity. The same information, however, also shows that this engine postdates the aircraft. Spitfire PR.IV, AB130, was taken on charge by the RAF on 23rd November 1941, but the engine was not despatched for service from the Rolls-Royce factory at Crewe until 4th April 1942. Another engine, with a remarkable documented history, shows an engine alone need not be a means to identifying an individual crash. This Merlin III, number 19281, was built at Derby by Rolls-Royce in February 1940. At the Supermarine factory in Southampton it was installed in Spitfire I, P9492, of No. 74 Squadron, on 29th March 1940. On 25th August it was removed, probably for overhaul. Once this was done, it was returned to service, this time in a Hurricane in late 1940, only to be removed for storage in April 1941. It found further work in another Hurricane in 1942, and then a Defiant, before a flying accident led to its removal, for the final time, on 28th June 1943. It survives to this day, intact, on display in Derby Industrial Museum. This sequence of engine changes, rarely so well recorded, shows that an engine might turn up in a crash but still be recorded as belonging to another aircraft on the record card.

It is also worth mentioning the prominent lettering marked on either side of the aircraft fuselage. These are conspicuous in photographs of contemporary aircraft (figure 7) but scarcely ever survive in aircraft

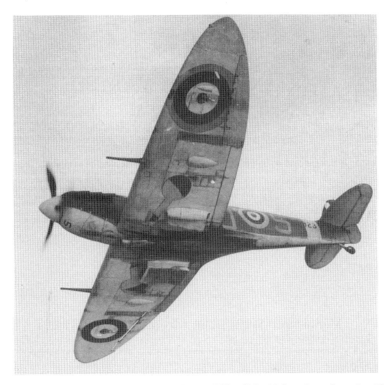

37. Spitfire V (in this case a modified Mark I), R6923, of No. 92 Squadron, flown by Allan Wright on 16th May 1941, photographed from a Blenheim for a series of publicity photographs. 'QJ' indicates the squadron, 'S' the aircraft (it was Wright's personal preference to transfer the letter 'S' to each aircraft he flew). Earlier in the war the squadron code was 'GR'.

wreckage, either because the airframe has been so damaged, or because the paint has been destroyed by chemical and water action. In the case of British aircraft, two letters normally marked the squadron, for example 'QJ' for No. 92 Squadron, and another letter distinguished the machine (figure 37). Sometimes, high-ranking individuals such as Douglas Bader were allowed to identify themselves. His aircraft were thus painted with the letters 'DB'. However, unlike aircraft serial numbers, these squadron codes could be (and were) transferred to replacement machines. American aircraft had similar arrangements (figure 31), but these were less strictly adhered to. Eventually a much wider range of colour codes was adopted for bombers so that crews could identify other machines of their groups. This was essential to make sure that the tight formations on which these daylight bombers depended for mutual defence could be

38. A B-17G tail bearing several different pieces of identifying information. The triangle indicates that the aircraft belongs to the First Bombardment Wing of the US Eighth Air Force. The letter K is the identifying code for the 379th Bombardment Group, and below that is the aircraft's individual serial number. This particular machine is displayed at Tulare, California, as a monument to the 379th. Although this machine never saw service in Britain, the markings are authentic.

maintained (figure 38). If any of these features turn up in excavations they can help narrow the process of tracing but they are unlikely to provide an exact identification.

Like any process of identification, tracking these serial numbers depends mainly on common sense. It is usually possible to identify an aircraft for certain but there remain many cases where confirmation has evaded excavators. The fact is that minute and rigorous examination of every part, as in the case of Trueman's Hurricane I, V6638, above, is the only reliable way to produce the information.

6
The airfields

The military airfields of Britain remain as the most visible relic of the air war but few now bear any resemblance to their wartime forms. They have been demolished and returned to agriculture, maintained as military or civil airfields, adapted for other uses and thus transformed beyond recognition, or been allowed to fall into decay. While the latter is the only way in which substantial authentic remains are likely to exist it is quite instructive for the archaeologist to see how the passage of only a few decades can reduce roadways to half-buried tracks and airfield buildings into barely recognisable tumbledown dereliction.

Britain is covered with the remains of old airfields but function and appearance were dictated by location, the tactics and grand strategy of aerial warfare, and the physical limitations of the machines. In the summer of 1940 a Spitfire I had a normal range of not much more than 640 km (400 miles). Even at a cruising speed of about 480 km/h (300 mph), it is clear that the aircraft did not have long in the air before needing refuelling. In combat range was vastly reduced, but, with only 15 seconds' worth of ammunition at first, the pilot might need to return to base to rearm anyway. German fighter aircraft were even worse off and also had to cross the English Channel first. Consequently, the principal fighter airfields are clustered around southern England, principally Sussex (such as Tangmere), Kent (such as Hawkinge and Biggin Hill) and Essex (such as Hornchurch and North Weald). It also happens to be the case that southern and eastern England is flatter than the rest of the British Isles and has thus lent itself to development for military aviation. Later in the war this would become a defining feature of the new bomber airfields built across East Anglia.

Even so, most of these airfields had been developed a generation before. This was achieved usually by requisitioning or purchasing farmland during the First World War (1914–18) to provide defences against the Zeppelin (airship) bombing raids and to provide support for ground forces fighting on the Western Front. After 1918 the new Royal Air Force found many of its bases being subjected to government cuts. It was decided that, for example, Hornchurch, Essex, would be returned to agriculture and its brand-new airfield buildings demolished. By the early 1920s this kind of decision was being reversed, and Hornchurch was reinstated. Other airfields were developed for civilian aviation. Croydon, Surrey, had been a First World War military airfield but between the wars it became London's principal airport. Out in north Kent, Gravesend was not even established until 1932, and then as an

39. The remains of the subterranean aviation-fuel dump at Hawkinge, Kent.

early attempt at providing London with an eastern airport. The coming of the Second World War meant reactivation of some airfields, development of existing ones such as Hornchurch and Kenley, and requisitioning for civilian fields like Gravesend. There were improvements and enlargements for almost all of them. Such complexes were also likely to include an operations room, control tower, fuel dumps (figure 39), ammunition stores, defensive installations (figure 40), a chapel, an education block, quarters for married staff, and separate

40. A pillbox (machine-gun post) at Hawkinge, Kent, is steadily encroached on by modern housing, which, at the time of writing, threatens to swamp the old airfield.

41. The officers' mess at Hawkinge in 1999. Built in 1937, this structure is now in advanced decay, despite renovation during the 1970s, and shows the first stages of how quickly a building can fall apart and become an archaeological feature in its own right.

mess facilities for officers and sergeants (figure 41). The art of defence against raids included dispersing aircraft around the airfield, protected by earthen mounds arranged on three sides at right angles. These fighter 'pens', joined by a perimeter road, helped restrict the effects of blast and could be very effective (figure 42). They survive at a number of wartime airfields.

42. A Spitfire I of No. 64 Squadron (SH-S) at Kenley surrounded by dust as a German raid on 18th August 1940 takes hold. The photograph was taken from one of the Dornier bombers as it flew overhead. Blast caused the Spitfire to rise up and collapse but it was otherwise protected by its pen. Many of these pens are visible today at wartime airfields.

Although the airfields were built for, and used by, aircraft, it is those aircraft that are now typically absent in any form. Many failed to return from combat while those that did could have been moved on elsewhere, crashed in training or scrapped at the end of the war. At Hawkinge conventional archaeological field-walking and surveying preceded house-building on the old airfield. Scarcely any artefacts associated with the aircraft were found, despite quantities of medieval and Roman pottery turning up. From a strictly archaeological point of view the airfield function would not have been recognised from the areas investigated, though buildings scattered around reveal the site's former function (figures 39–41) and subsequent excavations have turned up quantities of ammunition and fragments of aircraft.

At most of the surviving airfields at least some of these buildings are extant in some form today, though extremely few are preserved in a way which approximates to their appearance in 1940–1. Hornchurch was a front-line fighter base in 1940 but after the war it was abandoned to gravel extraction. The land has been refilled and preserved as a country park with the curious effect that it is still open grassland but several metres higher than it was in 1940. Around the perimeter wartime structures appear here and there, revealing its former function to the curious. At Biggin Hill modern light aircraft lurk in the pens once occupied by Spitfires and Hurricanes.

At the end of the war a few surviving aircraft were allocated to museums and some others made into 'gate guardians' (non-functional aircraft installed at the entrances to active airfields), a custom which survives but, as the value of intact Second World War aircraft steadily increases, these machines have now all been removed for either display indoors or full restoration to flying condition. The Spitfire XVI, TB752, presently on display in the museum at what was once RAF Manston, Kent, is one of the very few Spitfires with a genuine combat history residing on a former front-line fighter field. This very machine spent a night at Manston on active service in March 1945.

At all these airfields the principal feature was the landing and take-off area. At Kenley, Surrey, for example, the grass field was replaced in 1939 with the standard triangle of runways allowing for take-off and landing into whatever direction the wind was blowing. Some of the hangars had to be demolished and a local road diverted to make way for the new features. Not all fighter airfields were equipped with concrete runways, grass often being considered adequate. Westhampnett (now Chichester Goodwood) was left as a grass field, as it still is (figure 43).

Duxford, Cambridgeshire, was home to (amongst others) No. 19 Squadron, the first equipped with Spitfires, and later to the Thunderbolts of the USAAF 78th Fighter Group. Today it acts as the Imperial War Museum's

43. A Cessna 152 aircraft (flown by the author) at Chichester Goodwood airfield, formerly known as Westhampnett and home to the Spitfires of No. 602 (City of Glasgow) Squadron. The airfield is exceptional both in still being in use and in retaining grass landing strips as it had in the war.

principal repository of Second World War aircraft and is a major site for airshows. But it narrowly escaped strangulation by the building of the M11 motorway, and the essential installation of museum buildings has surrounded the wartime hangars with new facilities (figure 44).

44. B-17G Flying Fortress 44-83735, painted to represent *Mary Alice*, 42-31983, as displayed in the new American aircraft building at Duxford, Cambridgeshire. The real *Mary Alice* of the 401st Bombardment Group survived the war but was scrapped at Kingman, Arizona, in 1945.

45. A wartime hangar, now in civilian use, at the US Eighth Air Force base of Polebrook, Northamptonshire, where it housed B-17 Flying Fortresses of the 381st Bombardment Group (see also figure 50).

Part of the famous film *The Battle of Britain* (1968) was filmed at Duxford, re-enacting (without actually saying so) the real German raid on Kenley on 18th August 1940 (figure 42). Paradoxically, this outstanding effort to preserve the image and events of the Battle involved destroying some of the original evidence: many of today's flying Spitfires were restored to flying condition for the film (including the only Spitfire flying today that served in the Battle, the MKII, P7350), but one of Duxford's wartime hangars was blown up to create a spectacular climax to the re-enacted *Luftwaffe* raid. Other hangars at different locations now serve as light industrial accommodation or as farm buildings (figure 45). Similarly, the Nissen hut, that ubiquitous and swiftly erected building which served a thousand purposes, is today a structure that generations of pigs have cause to be grateful for.

By 1942 the air war was beginning to have different requirements. The RAF's four-engine heavy bomber, the Lancaster, was coming into service (figure 53). The USAAF had also arrived and needed huge numbers of bases for its four-engine bombers, the B-17 Flying Fortress (figures 31, 44) and the B-24 Liberator, as well as its medium bomber and fighter groups. This led to an explosion of airfield building throughout 1942 and 1943, mainly in East Anglia and Lincolnshire. The heavy bombers could operate reliably only from hard-surface runways. An American base was built from the outset around a triangle of three runways, the longest of which was 1.83 km (2000 yards) long, and the other two 1.28 km (1400 yards) long. Around these a continuous perimeter taxiway linked the runways and the buildings. Nearly 150,000 cubic metres (almost 200,000 cubic yards) of concrete were used, and it has been estimated that on average 1500 trees were removed to clear the site. Large numbers of buildings had to be erected, ranging from control towers to hangars, barracks, stores, kitchens and toilet facilities.

The RAF bomber fields are now largely redundant, though Coningsby, Lincolnshire, is home to the RAF Battle of Britain Memorial Flight. From here, the single British airworthy Lancaster I (PA474), *City of Lincoln,* still flies and the site is marked on maps as a heritage monument (figure 53). At East Kirkby, also in Lincolnshire, Lancaster VII (NX611), *Just Jane,* is regularly taxied on old runways. The American bases of the period have left some of the most visible remains but by 2000 this was increasingly dependent on deliberate preservation. Andrewsfield in Essex remains in use, with some wartime buildings, but the wartime concrete runways have been covered over with grass and only light aircraft land there now. At Thorpe Abbotts, Norfolk, the old base of the Eighth Air Force's 100th Bombardment Group, an enthusiastic group of local volunteers has preserved the control tower (figure 46). The runway is long gone but fragments of taxiway are visible, and ruinous airfield buildings lie scattered in surrounding woodland, a reminder of how susceptible these sites are to destruction in only a few decades (figures 41, 47). Preserving even a single building is expensive and

46. The restored control tower at Thorpe Abbotts, Norfolk, which overlooked the runway from which the B-17 Flying Fortresses of the US Eighth Air Force 100th Bombardment Group once took off.

47. Part of the taxiway complex at Thorpe Abbotts.

requires great enthusiasm. Not surprisingly few are now left. Motorists heading along the M11 motorway in Essex a few miles north of the junction with the M25 will notice that the road strikes right through the heart of North Weald airfield. The airfield is still active, but some hangars and other scattered buildings are visible on the other (west) side of the M11, rotting steadily away. Further north, on the A11, the modern road passes through Snetterton, Norfolk, which now serves as a racetrack, with a number of American wartime airfield buildings still extant and in use.

   The best means of researching airfields is to buy Ordnance Survey maps, where possible along with second-hand old one-inch editions. The latter will show many more airfields than modern maps, and by comparing the two it is possible to see where an airfield has been cleared away and where remnants may subsist. Visiting preserved sites like Thorpe Abbotts, Norfolk, and Framlingham, Suffolk, is a good start as active airfields like Biggin Hill, Kent, are not easily accessible to casual visitors and walkers. Elsewhere careful observation may reveal fragments of shattered concrete, left behind in fields when the runways were ripped up for use as hardcore. However, apart from public footpaths, right of access should not be assumed and permission should be sought from landowners before exploring in more detail.

7
Memorials

Most of the thousands of military air crashes in Britain before, during and after the Second World War, have long since been cleared away or are buried too deeply to be visible. Even some of those which are still detectable are too remote for easy access. Often, however, enthusiasts have seen fit to erect monuments to the aircraft and their crews and these now stand as poignant reminders to some of these tragedies. Many have been the result of excavations.

The selection of material used for the memorials varies. Often major components from the aircraft itself are used. At Aran Fawddwy near Bala in Gwynedd, Wales, a photo-reconnaissance de Havilland Mosquito from No. 540 Squadron, based at RAF Benson in Oxfordshire, crashed into the hills. As often happened, the crew failed to appreciate their height in poor weather and slammed into the peaks, scattering wreckage amongst the rocks, pools and bogs that cover the top of this windswept hill. There is effectively nothing left now on the crash site itself. But today, one of the Rolls-Royce Merlin engines resides, concreted into a plinth in a valley below to the west with a memorial plaque (figure 48).

48. Rolls-Royce Merlin twelve-cylinder engine from de Havilland Mosquito PR.XI, LR412, of No. 540 Squadron (RAF Benson, Oxfordshire). The fan device in the foreground is the supercharger which compensated for reduced air pressure at altitude. The aircraft crashed into Aran Fawddwy on 9th February 1944, killing both crew members. The engine is now displayed by a farm at Esgair-gawr off the A494 in the valley west of the crash site. It is itself a good example of the physical decay of aviation components. The alloy of the engine casing is disintegrating into powder, while the steel used for gears and the crankshaft is corroding steadily.

Other similar material used for this kind of memorial includes propeller blades. A blade from the B-24 Liberator which crashed in June 1945 into the Fairy Lochs (see chapter 1) is now set into a monument which also includes a brass plate, riveted into the rock surrounding the lake, that details the names of the crew and the passengers. In some instances, the blades were taken from crash sites at the time as trophies. Now they serve as memorials, for example a blade sawn from the wreckage of a Heinkel He 111 bomber which fell at Burgess Farm, Frittenden, Kent, on 15th September 1940, the date commemorated as Battle of Britain Day (figure 14).

These memorial plaques are sometimes the only evidence left on the crash site. A Vickers Wellington bomber from an RAF Officers' Training Unit crashed on Anglezarke Moor in the Pennines in November 1943. The site is now marked with a stone plinth bearing a square stone column with a plaque commemorating the crew. Another, exceptionally sad tragedy took place not far from the Mosquito crash at Aran Fawddwy mentioned above. Just after the end of the war in Europe a B-17G Flying Fortress carrying a crew of ten and ten passengers slammed into Craig Cwm Llydd, just south of Barmouth, Gwynedd, close to the Welsh coast. All twenty men were killed in the impact into an almost vertical hill face. There is scarcely anything left to mark the site today

49. Memorial to the B-17G Flying Fortress 44-8639 of the 351st Bombardment Group which crashed at Craig Cwm Llydd near Barmouth, Gwynedd, in June 1945. The plaque is at NGR SH 645122 (OS Landranger Sheet 124).

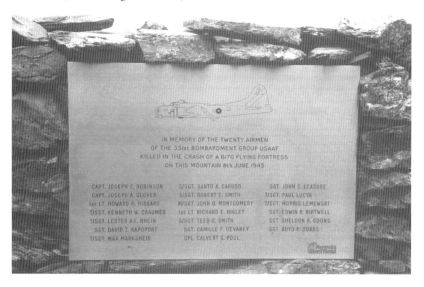

50. Memorial to the US Eighth Air Force 381st Bombardment Group at Polebrook, Northamptonshire. The monument sits on a full-width section of runway, most of which has now been cleared away to return the land to agriculture. Some airfield buildings survive (see figure 45).

except a stainless steel plaque located on the face of a field wall at the bottom of the steepest part of the slope (figure 49).

These memorials are explicit testimonials to aviation disasters. More general monuments to the air war can be found all round Britain, usually recording specific units on their airfields. At Polebrook in Northamptonshire, for example, the US Eighth Air Force 381st Bombardment Group is commemorated on a stone which belongs to the great tradition of military memorials (figure 50). In time it may be the only evidence of the unit's presence, though for the moment it stands on a small part of the airfield runway in sight of a wartime hangar still in civilian use (figure 45). This is an interesting example of the process of an archaeological feature developing. For the moment the inscription is in context, in the setting for which it was designed. In the centuries to come it may be damaged, moved or lost altogether, only to resurface

Aviation Archaeology in Britain

51. The grave of Pilot Officer Charles Woods-Scawen at Folkestone Cemetery, Hawkinge, Kent. He was killed when he baled out too low from his burning Hurricane but none of this is recorded on the tombstone.

one day when its original location is lost.

Less obvious, but far more numerous, are the graves of the aircrew which are widely distributed in military and public cemeteries across Britain. Many of the American aircrew are buried at Madingley Cemetery near Cambridge, while RAF crew tend to be more widely dispersed, sometimes with plots adjacent to those of German aircrew, for example at Folkestone Cemetery, which lies next to the old airfield at Hawkinge. These provide little more than the most basic information such as the pilot's name, his age and date of death. The grave of Pilot Officer Charles Woods-Scawen is easy to find today at Hawkinge. It tells us that he died on 2nd September 1940 at the age of twenty-two but nothing about how he came to be killed (figure 51). Searching through the available records, the story emerges. Charles Woods-Scawen flew Hawker Hurricanes with No. 43 Squadron out of Tangmere, way to the west near Chichester. On 2nd September at around lunchtime his squadron found itself fighting Messerschmitt Bf 109s over eastern Kent. Woods-Scawen's machine caught fire in the melee and he attempted to force-land his doomed aircraft. It seems that he decided he had no chance of making it and baled out. Unfortunately he was too low and he

52. Spitfire IX, MH434. This machine served with No. 222 Squadron in the Second World War and bears that squadron's code, ZD, to commemorate the fact. It now spends its time being flown in displays at air shows.

was killed. His aircraft, V7420, was later excavated and its remains recovered by Brenzett Museum.

Such graves are interesting artefacts in their own right. They are admirable in their simplicity and modest conformity but one day will form part of the long-term archaeological record of our era. Without the associated documentation the stone provides little information and to most visitors to the cemetery today these details are already far from evident. Indeed, Roman tombstones often provide more detailed information and usually include details of a soldier's unit and length of service, his family and his place of origin.

As living memory of this period begins to fade, the physical memorials become all the more important but many aircraft serving as commemorations of the air war in Europe are rare and widely dispersed. Spitfire IX, MH434, is one of the British-based airworthy Spitfires. It has a genuine combat history with No. 222 Squadron but has spent most of its life since it was used in the 1968 *Battle of Britain* film appearing on the air show circuit (figure 52). The RAF Battle of Britain Memorial Flight's airworthy Avro Lancaster, PA474, did not serve in the war itself though it is routinely painted in the squadron markings of examples which did, by way of commemoration (figure 53). Several other non-airworthy Lancasters survive in Britain but only one of these was used by RAF Bomber Command during the war (R5868, now at Hendon). The sheer scarcity may not be easily appreciated but at the end of the war aircraft were scrapped so hastily that the lead aircraft used by Wing-Commander Guy Gibson in the celebrated Dams Raid of May 1943, Lancaster ED932, was destroyed along with many other less

53. Lancaster I, PA474, of the Battle of Britain Memorial Flight, towers over crowds. Although this machine never saw war service, it provides a useful link between history, aviation archaeology and the present by being the only airworthy example of this machine in Europe.

notable machines. The water tanks used by the designer of the bouncing bomb, Barnes Wallis, were also demolished in 1997 without announcement or ceremony, which highlights how much has disappeared in a few decades.

The only currently airworthy Spitfire which saw service in the Battle of Britain, the Mk II P7350, was sent for scrap after the war. The scrap merchant fortunately recognised the aircraft's pedigree and returned it to the RAF. Most airworthy aircraft of the period are restored examples from later in the war (figure 3). The small number of other surviving aircraft from the Battle of Britain period reside in museums. While it does not seem surprising to describe Roman or medieval artefacts as unique it is sobering to realise that some Second World War aircraft are now non-existent, such as the Short Stirling bomber.

This state of affairs has led to a new dimension in aviation archaeology. Restorations and reconstructions have become familiar activities in other branches of archaeology, as a means to understanding lost techniques. Raising Egyptian obelisks, or moving Stonehenge-sized blocks, are amongst the most popular. This too has become a feature of aviation archaeology. Recovery and excavation of a moderately intact, but wrecked, aircraft is followed by painstaking replacement of almost all components (using the old as templates) while retaining the machine's original serial number. The process harnesses skills surviving amongst men and women who once worked in wartime factories, and which have been learned by some aviation archaeologists using their experience to run businesses manufacturing new components for wartime aircraft. The process illustrates how aviation archaeology has combined

54. Bristol Beaufighter 21, A8-324, of the Royal Australian Air Force being rebuilt at Duxford, Cambridgeshire, from wreckage found in the Far East.

excavation with restoration and re-enactment, creating artefacts which function as they were once supposed to. At Duxford a Bristol Beaufighter was nearing completion to flying condition in 2000 (figure 54). This type has not flown for decades and, although the question of 'originality' with all such restorations is controversial, this work enables a modern audience to experience something of a living past.

8
Further reading

The number of books dealing with military aviation of the Second World War is colossal and increasing all the time. Few, however, are concerned with aviation archaeology in its various manifestations. The following include examples of useful general works, and others more specifically concerned with tracing crash sites and researching the surrounding circumstances.

Baxter, G. G., Owen, K. A., and Baldock, P. *Aircraft Casualties in Kent; Part 1, 1939 to 1940.* Meresborough Books, 1990.
Bédoyère, G. de la. *Battles over Britain. The Archaeology of the Air War.* Tempus, 2000.
Bowyer, M. J. F. *Aircraft for the Few.* Patrick Stephens, 1991.
Bowyer, M. J. F. *Aircraft for the Many.* Patrick Stephens, 1995.
Brooks, R. J. *Kent Airfields in the Second World War.* Countryside Books, 1998.
Deighton, L. *The Battle of Britain.* Jonathan Cape, 1980.
Ellis, K. *Aviation Museums of Britain.* Midland Publishing, 1995.
Ellis, K. *Wrecks and Relics.* Midland Publishing, various annual updates.
Franks, N. L. R. *Royal Air Force Fighter Command Losses of the Second World War; Volume 1, Operational Losses: Aircraft and Crews 1939–1941.* Midland Publishing, 1997. (Other volumes by this author in the series complete the war years.)
Freeman, R. A. *Airfields of the Eighth.* After the Battle, 1978.
Freeman, R. A. *The Fight for the Skies.* Arms and Armour, 1998.
Gibson, G. *Enemy Coast Ahead.* Michael Joseph, 1946 (and numerous reprints).
Harvey-Bailey, A. *The Merlin in Perspective: The Combat Years.* Rolls-Royce Heritage Trust, fourth edition 1995.
Hillary, R. *The Last Enemy.* Macmillan, 1942 (frequently reprinted).
Hough, R., and Richards, D. *The Battle of Britain.* Hodder & Stoughton, 1989.
Jackson, R. *Spitfire. The Combat History.* Airlife, 1995.
Kaplan, P., and Collier, R. *The Few: Summer, 1940: The Battle of Britain.* Greenwich Editions, 1996.
McLachlan, I. *Final Flights.* Patrick Stephens, 1989.
Mondey, D. *British Aircraft of World War II.* Chancellor Press, 1994.
Mondey, D. *Axis Aircraft of World War II.* Chancellor Press, 1996.
Morgan, E. B., and Shacklady, E. *Spitfire: The History.* Key Publishing, 1987.
Price, A. *Spitfire: A Documentary History.* Macdonald & Jane's, 1977.
Price, A. *The Hardest Day.* Macdonald & Jane's, 1979.
Price, A. *The Spitfire Story.* Arms & Armour, second edition 1995.
Ramsey, W. G. (editor). *The Blitz Then and Now; Volume 1, September 3, 1939 – September 6, 1940.* After the Battle Magazine, 1987.
Ramsey, W. G. (editor). *The Blitz Then and Now; Volume 2, September 7, 1940 – May 1941.* After the Battle Magazine, 1989.
Ramsey, W. G. (editor). *The Battle of Britain Then and Now.* After the Battle Magazine, fifth edition 1989.

Ramsey, W. G. (editor). *The Blitz Then and Now; Volume 3, May 1941 – May 1945.* After the Battle Magazine, 1990.

Shaw, P. *Discover Aviation Trails: Touring Britain's Aviation Heritage.* Midland Publishing, 1996.

Smith, D. J. *High Ground Wrecks and Relics.* Midland Publishing, fourth edition 1997.

Stevens, S. G. L. 'Archaeological Investigations at Hawkinge Aerodrome, Hawkinge, Kent' (forthcoming).

Terraine, J. *The Right of Line: The Royal Air Force in the European War 1939–1945.* Hodder & Stoughton, 1985.

Townshend Bickers, R. *The Battle of Britain.* Ted Smart, 1990.

9
Museums

Although the major museums are generally open all year round, many of the small local aviation museums (marked *) are open only on limited dates during the summer season, so it is advisable to telephone in advance before making a special journey. During the summer months there are also air shows at numerous venues around Britain where airworthy machines from the war years can be seen. Dates are publicised in magazines such as *Flypast* and *Aeroplane*. Amongst the most popular are Biggin Hill in Kent, Duxford in Cambridgeshire and Fairford in Gloucestershire, though there are many others.

Battle of Britain Memorial Flight, RAF Coningsby, Coningsby, Lincolnshire LN4 4SY. Telephone: 01526 344041. Website: www.bbmf.co.uk (Historic aircraft on display depend on which are away attending air shows.)
Brenzett Aeronautical Museum Trust*, Ivychurch Road, Brenzett, Romney Marsh, Kent TN29 0EE. Telephone: 01233 627911.
De Havilland Aircraft Heritage Centre*, PO Box 107, Salisbury Hall, London Colney, St Albans, Hertfordshire AL2 1BU. Telephone: 01727 822051.
Derby Industrial Museum, Full Street, Derby DE1 3AR. Telephone: 01332 255308. Website: www.derby.gov.uk/museums
Imperial War Museum, Duxford Airfield, Duxford, Cambridgeshire CB2 4QR. Telephone: 01223 835000. Website: www.iwm.org.uk
Imperial War Museum, Lambeth Road, London SE1 6HZ. Telephone: 020 7416 5320. Website: www.iwm.org.uk
Kent Battle of Britain Museum*, Aerodrome Road, Hawkinge, Folkestone, Kent CT18 7AG. Telephone: 01303 893140.
Lashenden Air Warfare Museum*, Headcorn Aerodrome, near Ashford, Kent TN27 9HX. Telephone: 01622 890226.
Lincolnshire Aviation Heritage Centre, East Kirkby, near Spilsby, Lincolnshire PE23 4DE. Telephone: 01790 763207.
Manston Spitfire and Hurricane Memorial Building, The Airfield, Manston Road, Ramsgate, Kent CT12 5BS. Telephone: 01843 821940. Website: www.spitfire-museum.com
Parham (Framlingham) 390th Bomb Group Memorial Air Museum*, Parham, Suffolk (information from 101 Avondale Road, Ipswich, Suffolk IP3 9LA). Telephone: 01473 711275.
Royal Air Force Museum, Cosford, Shifnal, Shropshire TF11 8UP. Telephone: 01902 374112. Website: www.rafmuseum.com
Royal Air Force Museum, Grahame Park Way, Hendon, London NW9 5LL. Telephone: 020 8205 2266. Website: www.rafmuseum.com
Science Museum, Exhibition Road, South Kensington, London SW7 2DD. Telephone: 020 7938 8080. Website: www.sciencemuseum.org.uk
Shoreham Aircraft Museum*, High Street, Shoreham Village, Sevenoaks, Kent TN14 7TB. Telephone: 01959 524416. Website: www.s-a-m.freeserve.co.uk
Shuttleworth Collection, Old Warden Park, Biggleswade, Bedfordshire SG18 9EA. Telephone: 01767 627288. Website: www.shuttleworth.co.uk
Tangmere Military Aviation Museum*, Tangmere, near Chichester, West Sussex PO20 6ES. Telephone: 01243 775223.
Thorpe Abbotts, 100th Bombardment Group Association*, Common Road, Dickleburgh, Diss, Norfolk IP21 4PH. Telephone: 01379 740708.
Yorkshire Air Museum*, Halifax Way, Elvington, near York YO41 4AU. Telephone: 01904 608595. Website: www.yorkairmuseum.freeserve.co.uk

Index

Page numbers in italics refer to illustrations